# IT'S TIME TO LEARN ABOUT BEAGLE DOGS

# It's Time to Learn about Beagle Dogs

Walter the Educator

Silent King Books
A WhichHead Entertainment Imprint

Copyright © 2025 by Walter the Educator

All rights reserved. No part of this book may be reproduced in any manner whatsoever without written per- mission except in the case of brief quotations embodied in critical articles and reviews.

First Printing, 2024

Disclaimer

This book is a literary work; the story is not about specific persons, locations, situations, and/or circumstances unless mentioned in a historical context. Any resemblance to real persons, locations, situations, and/or circumstances is coincidental. This book is for entertainment and informational purposes only. The author and publisher offer this information without warranties expressed or implied. No matter the grounds, neither the author nor the publisher will be accountable for any losses, injuries, or other damages caused by the reader's use of this book. The use of this book acknowledges an understanding and acceptance of this disclaimer.

It's Time to Learn about Beagle Dogs is a collectible early learning book by Walter the Educator suitable for all ages belonging to Walter the Educator's Time to Eat Book Series. Collect more books at WaltertheEducator.com

**USE THE EXTRA SPACE TO TAKE NOTES AND DOCUMENT YOUR MEMORIES**

# BEAGLE DOGS

The Beagle is a dog so sweet,

# It's Time to Learn about
# Beagle Dogs

With floppy ears and speedy feet.

A nose that sniffs both low and high,

It finds a scent and runs right by!

Their fur is short in white and brown,

Or black and tan all spread around.

Their tails stick up, so bright and bold,

Like flags they wave as stories unfold!

Beagles love to sniff and chase,

Through open fields, they dash with grace.

They track down scents both old and new,

Their noses tell them what to do!

A Beagle's bark is loud and strong,

They howl and sing a Beagle song.

They love to talk and let you know,

When something's near or time to go!

# It's Time to Learn about
# Beagle Dogs

They're friendly dogs, both smart and kind,

With loving hearts and clever minds.

They wag their tails and run to play,

With energy to last all day!

They love their food, they'll beg and sneak,

For treats or bites, they'll even peek!

But careful not to overfeed,

A healthy pup is what they need.

A Beagle loves to dig and run,

Exploring trails is so much fun!

But watch them close or they may stray,

Their noses lead them far away!

They cuddle close when day is done,

A Beagle's love is never gone.

They rest their heads upon your knee,

# It's Time to Learn about
# Beagle Dogs

A perfect friend for you and me!

They need long walks, they need some space,

To run and sniff and stretch and race.

So if you love to walk and roam,

A Beagle makes the perfect home!

So if you see a Beagle pup,

With nose to ground and tail straight up,

Just know this dog is brave and true,

# It's Time to Learn about
# Beagle Dogs

And wants to be a friend to you!

# ABOUT THE CREATOR

Walter the Educator is one of the pseudonyms for Walter Anderson. Formally educated in Chemistry, Business, and Education, he is an educator, an author, a diverse entrepreneur, and he is the son of a disabled war veteran. "Walter the Educator" shares his time between educating and creating. He holds interests and owns several creative projects that entertain, enlighten, enhance, and educate, hoping to inspire and motivate you. Follow, find new works, and stay up to date with Walter the Educator™ at WaltertheEducator.com

www.ingramcontent.com/pod-product-compliance
Lightning Source LLC
LaVergne TN
LVHW052017060526
838201LV00059B/4072